UNLEASHED LIBATIONS

CANINES & COCKTAILS

RABBIT HOUSE PRESS
Versailles, KY 40383

Copyright © 2020 by Sara Don Shaver

Published in the United States by Rabbit House Press, February 2021.
Printed in the United States of America.

For inquiries about author appearances and/or volume orders, please visit www.rabbithousepress.com

Back cover photo: Iverson "Norm" Shaver
Cocktail photos: Hillary Truelove
Editor: Erin Chander
Cover & interior design: Brooke Lee

ISBN: 978-1-7351727-4-3

Unleashed Libations

Canines & Cocktails

Sara Don Shaver

CONTENTS

INTRODUCTION

I may not be the supreme expert at either, but my passion, knowledge and experience make me pretty damn good at both. I am aware that to most people making drinks and training dogs don't inherently go hand in hand; however, if you have ever spent a day—or even 5 minutes—training a dog or owner that proves to be a challenge, you know that a frosty beverage is sometimes... lots of times... the best remedy.

As I sit with a freshly shaken martini after a day of successful and not so successful training sessions, owners from one extreme to the other, I realize this book is long overdue... even if only for my personal sanity. Training a dog comes with so many ups and downs, good memories and sad, challenges and triumphs, but in the end is worth every second spent! Whether you have a success or setback, shaking up a cocktail helps celebrate the former or gives you an outlet to get the desired result in cases of the latter.

I love to make fancy drinks with fancy ingredients, and it is fun to teach dogs fancy tricks. This book contains neither. It is filled with easy to use tips and easy to follow recipes with accessible ingredients. When executed properly, both sides of this equation will make your day a bit more enjoyable. Let's be honest, even if the recipes aren't executed properly, they will still likely make your day a bit more enjoyable.

This is meant to be helpful and fun. This is NOT a training manual. These are useful, helpful tips... NOT guarantees... almost usually's, NOT absolutes. Train up, mix up and drink up... responsibly! *Cheers!*

No dogs consumed any alcohol in the making of this book... lots of humans did.

A FEW THINGS FOR THE BAR

* 2 oz Jigger

    I bought one to create this book... yes, I'm that good.
* Bar Spoon
* Small cutting board
* Paring knife
* Fine mesh cocktail strainer
* 4 prong bar strainer
* Muddler
* Bar towels

    Nice to have handy for splashes and spills.
* Cocktail shaker

    I prefer a Boston Shaker.
* Light Agave
* Bitterman's Habanero Shrub

* Blood Orange Shrub
* Bitters

> See recipes... get lots and experiment!

* Small colander

> To discard muddled fruit and such.

* Sugar Cubes
* Veggie Peeler
* Cocktail Garnish Picks

BRANDIED CHERRIES

Pitted Bing Cherries (buy a pitter... they rock)

> 1.5 C Brandy
>
> 1/3 C Sugar
>
> 1/2 C Water

Fill pint mason jars with cherries. Mix Brandy, sugar and water in a small saucepan over medium heat until sugar dissolves. Pour over cherries and put on lids. Let cool and refrigerate until needed.

I like to let them sit for at least a week before I begin using them!

Sara Don Shaver

TIP #1

Let's start with one simple, yet extremely important concept to remember when training dogs: consistency is key! At its core, training is repetition of any task until the muscles and brain react automatically upon receiving a certain stimulus. Any variance in commands or gestures used will create confusion in your dog's brain. Leeway given on your part will give your dog the impression you do not mean what you say when you say it.

Your dog will naturally salivate. However, they must be conditioned to sit at the door patiently waiting for you to let them outside to relieve themselves. This only comes through diligence on your part, the unyielding commitment to gain the dog's attention, instruct them, and correct negative behavior or reward a positive result, over and over and over until it's second nature. Even older, trained dogs may need a refresher session every now and then to reel them in when they decide to look at you with that "screw you, I know I'm cute so I'm going to pretend I don't understand what you're saying," face.

Quite simply, if you do not train your dog, he or she will not be trained! Got it?

If so, you may now train yourself by following the recipe on the next page. Mix, sip, enjoy, and repeat as necessary until you've mastered the concept of consistency or you forget what day it is and that your dog has been waiting patiently by the back door for 45 minutes!

DUKE'S DRAFTY GIN

2.5 oz. Floral Gin such as a St. George or Hendrick's Variety

1 oz. Dry Vermouth

1 Hooegarden or other hefeweizen-style beer

Rosemary sprig

   (easiest if you take it off the woody stem for muddling)

Lemon Wedge

Muddle rosemary and lemon wedge in glass part of shaker. Top with ice. Add gin and vermouth. Cap with tin part of shaker, shake vigorously and strain into a mule or glass mug filled with ice. Top with beer and garnish with a lemon twist and rosemary sprig. Duke looked strong and bold, yet was unexpectedly gentle and easy... just like this cocktail.

Cheers!

DUKE

TIP #2

Take the human out. By that I mean leave your feelings and desire to converse with your dog at the door. Thinking back to Tip #1, training is a matter of consistency. Any extraneous words or actions you throw into the mix only serve to confuse. Praise the manners you wish to continue and in some circumstances ignore those you do not, but do both in a concise and compassionately authoritative manner.

If your dog is barking or jumping at you, don't have a five minute conversation with them to explain how their behavior is negatively impacting your day. Your words make you feel better and make self-affirming sense to you, but will most likely be interpreted as you giving the dog attention, which is what caused them to jump or bark in the first place. Have you ever noticed how your dog acts when someone comes over for a visit? Out of an innate sense of curiosity, your dog will approach your guest who probably responds by quickly patting the dog's head and then saying something to the effect of "okay, now go away" while lightly pushing with their hand over and over. The dog interprets this as attention, increasing interest and the desire to remain in the situation. In response, you and your guest become increasingly agitated and verbose creating an emotionally charged environment and inadvertently fueling the dog's fire.

The appropriate response in the preceding situation would be to have your dog sit and stay. Subsequently, instruct your guests to do the same. If neither complies, put your dog on a leash to extend your control of the situation. You can also simply remove the dog to their crate or a different room with an appropriate chewing distraction. Create an easy non-stressful situation for all... hence, "take the human out."

HANNIBAL

HANNIBAL'S HABANRITA

3 oz Reposado Tequila

1 oz Citronge

Juice of 1 Lime

Juice of about ¼ Orange

Squirt to taste of Light Agave

Egg White

Bitterman's Hellfire Habanero Shrub

Mix all ingredients except the Habanero Shrub in shaker with NO ICE and shake vigorously. HOLD TIGHT as the seal may break and release a delicious mess. Add the ice and shake vigorously again. Strain with strainer and shaker tin in one hand into the mesh strainer held slightly above a Large Coupe or Margarita glass. When shaker is empty tap the mesh strainer to release the accumulated egg white foam. Top with ½ dropper of Habanero Shrub (adjust to heat tolerance). Garnish with a twist of lime or orange and fresh habanero. Taste the complex perfection of one of the best drinks you'll ever have... just like Hannibal was one of the best dogs!

TIP #3

Part of your relationship with your dog starts from your end of the leash. This is why it is important to keep a controlled walk. If you let your dog zig zag, pull, stop, etc., he is in control. That will permeate into all aspects of life with your pooch. Don't let them be in control. They go where you decide they can go. If he pulls one way and drags you along, he will be a puller. You being in control doesn't make the walk less enjoyable for the dog, just more enjoyable for you. It also sets you on a path for a more cohesive relationship. If you have a rude walker and use a retractable leash, take that bulky leash handle and knock yourself in the noggin. Hopefully, common sense has kicked in and you realize why this is counterproductive and dangerous. If you actually have a safely controlled, well behaved dog on a retractable leash... let's think really hard and be honest with yourself, you deserve a few of the following rewards. As a professional, I have seen almost none... nope none! That was me thinking really hard and honestly. Now I may drink!

TIP #6

Your dog is going to feed off your confidence and energy. If there is a new situation, new noises, thunderstorms, or the like, and your dog seems unsure or afraid, don't coddle them. When you lower your body and voice as if to say, "oh you poor guy, it's okay," you are making yourself feel better. In reality, this makes the dog feel as if they should react that way in those situations. Be upbeat, confident and encouraging as if to say, "Let's go... it's all good." If you have a puppy, begin exposure to new people, sounds and environments early and you will avoid a lot of issues from developing or progressing. If you are dealing with a grown dog, they may have issues triggered from past experiences. A similar approach a little at a time will help. You clearly shouldn't toss a quiet country dog into the middle of NYC rush hour or a dog that shies away from kids into the middle of a daycare. Sip by sip is how we make progress. Chugging never has the most desired outcome!

BULLY BLOODY TINI

2 oz Tito's

½ oz Noilly Prat Dry Vermouth

1.5 oz Tomato Juice

Dash of Worcestershire Sauce

Dash of Horseradish

Fresh or dried Dill

Celery Seed

Squeeze of Lime

Bitterman's Hellfire Habanero Shrub

Add all ingredients except Shrub to a shaker with ice and shake. Strain with a mesh strainer into a martini glass. Top with several drops of the Shrub. Garnish with an assortment of your faves. I'm a fan of fresh cucumber, fresh tomato, garlic stuffed olive and cocktail onion. I think it makes a better balance when you have some fresh and some pickled.

TIP #7

Not to harp on the issue, but I am going to harp on an issue... your energy! Most anxieties are created by humans when you get a dog as a puppy. For rescues, it may be less than stellar owners or situations of the past. Stop projecting your self-gratifying words and feelings onto them. With each "oh, I'm sorry I am putting you in this crate..." and "oh, come here, I will save you from that thunder," it simply makes you feel better and only exacerbates an issue that can easily not be one. It is doing an injustice to the dog, not "loving" them more. You are creating the problem!

No long goodbyes. When you are leaving, just put them in the crate and close it up possibly with a treat to top it off... and leave! If there is storm, no biggie. Just toss a ball or something else to redirect focus. Think about how much more chill and happy your dog's life will be if you don't constantly try to make yourself feel better... and surprise! It will make you feel better because you won't have the issue!

SISI'S MIST

2 oz Tito's Vodka

½ oz Cointreau

Sugar cube

Regan's Orange Bitters

Lemon Wedges

Lemon or Tangerine White Claw or your favorite hard seltzer

Soak a sugar cube with the bitters and muddle with two lemon wedges. Add ice, vodka and Cointreau. Shake and strain over ice in a Collins style glass. Top with the hard seltzer and garnish with slice of orange. For a different twist, use brandied cherry juice in addition or instead of the Cointreau and add a brandied cherry for garnish. Sierra (Sisi) is an unknown mix that has added so much fluff and excitement to our lives just as this drink will do for your guests!

TIP #8

Have your dog's attention before spouting off commands. As a whole, there are exceptions amongst breeds, if your dog isn't looking at you, he isn't hearing you. Make a noise or say their name, then give the command. Commands need to be given when you know the dog will follow through. Otherwise, they lose their meaning. This means, WORK WITH YOUR DOG! Working doesn't have to take 30 minutes at a time. Take a second here and there. Turn play time into training time. If you put the word with the action over and over, guess what, it becomes a command. If you haven't trained your dog to do it, stop telling them to do it! People like to make themselves look good in public, as if they train their dogs, saying, "sit, come, stop jumping... " but it is actually wasting their breath and annoying everyone around them. I say again with different words, TRAIN YOUR DOG! Got it?

REDFORD, RIVER, BITTY GIRL

CAVI CABARET

Absinthe

2oz Dry Gin such as Plymouth or Sapphire

½ oz Dolin Dry Vermouth

½ oz Benedictine

2 dashes Peyschaud's Bitters

2 dashes Reagan's Orange Bitters

Swirl a drop of Absinthe in a coupe glass. Add all ingredients in shaker over ice. Stir with a bar spoon for about 20 seconds until it seems right. Strain into the coupe glass and garnish with two brandied cherries and a twist of lemon after releasing the oil and rubbing on the rim of the glass. Sip away with the class and sass of a Cavi!

TIP #9

Get your friends, family and strangers on board with your training goals. Don't hesitate to tell them not to pet your pooch until it is sitting or calm with all feet on the ground. Sometimes the people we encounter can be the biggest undoing of our training efforts. This doesn't mean your dog can't get attention or people can't engage, but let's make it a more respectful and polite interaction on both sides. Your dog, your rules... think about what you want in the long run!

ATTILA

ATTILA'S APEROL

2 oz Aperol

½ oz Tito's Vodka

½ oz Dry Vermouth

Prosecco

Orange twist

Build over ice in a Collins style glass or Aluminum cup. Express an orange twist over the drink and swirl around the rim of the glass. That's it! Just like our Attila, this drink is easy and strong... not as passive as it seems.

For a party: Take a few oranges and slice about ¼ inch thick. Stack in single layers between wax paper and freeze overnight. Use one bottle Aperol, ¼ or so bottle of Vermouth, ¼ bottle of Tito's, four bottles of Prosecco. Put all ingredients in a fancy drink dispenser. Drop in the frozen oranges and serve!

TIP #10

Know your dog's elimination schedule! This is essential to successful house training. If you have no clue when they have gone 'number one' or 'number two,' you won't be able to determine if they should have some free playtime or if they should be under lockdown in order not to soil your expensive rug. If you know what times of day your dog will typically poop, and they have not gone an hour or so past the norm... crate them or Velcro them to you and try again in 10-15 minutes. Repeat this until successful.

If you don't do this while establishing a schedule and learning your dog's needs, they will undoubtedly go inside. All dogs will have accidents at some stage, but try to keep it to as few as possible. Be aware of what is going in and what is coming out. If you don't actually see them pee... did they? Just because they spent time outside, does not mean they did the job. Knowing the finished poop structure (i.e. tapered end or solid to softer) will help you know if they are actually finished going. The same with pee as some dogs double pee. If they don't get that second part in before you think they are done, guess where it ends up. Most dogs get to a stage where you won't have to be as aware, but until they prove that... BE AWARE!

Enough about excrement, have a drink!

TIP #11

Your dog is not a robot. If you want a robot, buy a robot. In this day and age there should be a plethora of options for you to choose from.

DUKE

MOSCOW WATCHDOG

2 oz Tito's Vodka

1 oz Domaine De Canton Ginger Liquor

Lime Bitters

Fresh Ginger

Lime wedge

Soda Water

Muddle a lime wedge and about ¼ inch of fresh ginger. Add ice and the liquors and shake vigorously. Strain into a mule mug filled with fresh ice. Top with soda water, garnish with a lime wedge and strip of fresh ginger. Top with a few dashes of lime bitters. Strong and sneaky. Take note of how many you consume as they go down easy!

TIP #12

Ask yourself: "Am I going this way because I decided to go this way, or am I being dragged by my dog? Did I give a reward for something I asked for or wish to encourage or am I giving into a demand?" Everything needs to be on your terms. Rewards and praise are earned, and believe me, when your dog learns what it gets those for... it does it as a default. If you do what your dog demands by barking, jumping or pulling, you will have a bratty bossy dog that may not "love" you quite as much as you think. A relationship is deeper when not one sided, so build one by building structure together.

WINEY WEIMY

3 oz. Blanco Tequila

1 oz. Cointreau

Juice of 1 Lime

Juice from an Orange and Lemon wedge

1 small squirt of light agave

1 oz. Grenache or other dry Spanish Red wine

Add all ingredients except the wine in a shaker filled with ice. Shake and strain into a Highball type glass filled with fresh ice. Leave about ½ inch of room. Take your bar spoon with the rounded side up next to the edge of the glass and slowly pour the wine over it creating a separate layer. Garnish with an orange wheel.

TIP #13

Every dog is unique and has its own quirks, tendencies and personality. Just because you have had dogs, done it this way, "my old dog didn't do this..." does not mean it will be the same with your current dog. It is not a one size fits all approach. Sometimes alterations are needed. Pay attention as you may need to change your approach to succeed. You also may have to accept that your old way may not be the right way... for this dog. Finding a new approach can be fun and easy. Broaden your horizons!

CHIVAS

RIVER

TIP #14

Remove interest in off limits places and things by simply removing access to them. If the chair leg was never an option as a chew toy, it will not be the desired option as a chew toy. This means as stated in tip #5, he was never alone long enough to get a taste of the chair leg. If your dog isn't supposed to go upstairs, get a gate so they can't get up there. If you don't want them on the couch in the long run, don't let them on the couch ever. Create what you expect. If they don't have access, they won't have interest!

Seems simple, right? It is!

AFFINITY FOR CHIVAS

1.5 oz Chivas Regal

½ oz Sweet Vermouth

½ oz Dry Vermouth

Boker's Bitters

Twist of Orange

Add the liquors and bitters over ice and stir about 30 rounds. Strain into a stemmed glass. Express and swirl a twist of orange for garnish. Chivas may have only had three legs just like this cocktail has three liquors, but he never skipped a beat or lacked in any way and neither does this. Sometimes simple and few makes something more unique and pleasing!

TIP #15

A crate is a useful training tool. If you use it as punishment, you should definitely not have a dog. If you ONLY see it as punishment and not a useful training tool, you should quite possibly not have a dog. It is their space, and when used properly will be a haven for them. Don't get the proper uses for a crate mixed up with the improper uses. Let's be realistic.

REDFORD

Fashionable Sundance

3 oz Bulleit Rye

½ oz Blood Orange Shrub

A few dashes of Boker's Bitters

Mix all ingredients over ice and stir with a bar spoon until it feels about right. Strain into highball glass with an ice sphere. Garnish with a brandied cherry or two and a twist of orange. This cocktail is distinguished, classic and smooth... just like its namesake, Redford.

WHISKEY'S SMASH

    2 oz Wild Turkey Longbranch Bourbon

    1 oz Dry Vermouth

    Fresh mint leaves (about 6)

    Lemon Wedge

    Bitters

    Sugar cube

Soak the sugar cube in bitters and muddle with about five mint leaves and a lemon wedge. Add ice and liquor and shake until your shaker starts to frost. Strain into an old-fashioned style glass with an ice sphere or large cube. Slap a mint leaf and place in cocktail along with a twist of expressed lemon twist. Just like my boy Whiskey, this drink is quintessential and cool... better than the standard!

WHISKEY

BITTY GIRL BASILINI

3 Basil Leaves

3 Blackberries

1.5 oz Tito's Vodka

1 oz St. Germain Elderflower Liquor

Champagne (I like Brut)

Muddle the basil and blackberries and top with ice. Add the Tito's and St. Germain. Shake and strain through a mesh strainer into a stemmed glass such as a large coupe. Top with Champagne and garnish with lemon twist, a smacked basil leaf and float a blackberry. Just like Lizzie, my Bitty Girl, this drink is perfectly beautiful and compelling!

BITTY GIRL

I hope you take time to train your dog, walk your dog and play with your dog. Dogs add so much to our lives so add to theirs. Make a good life for them. Be good to them and love them. Earn their affection in positive ways while helping them be the best and happiest they can be. So much of what we blame on dogs is actually the human's doing. It is almost always (I said almost) our fault. Accept responsibility and grow with your dog. Build a cohesive relationship. When in doubt seek a professional! Small things can turn to big things that are much harder to fix the longer they go on. Goals are much more rewarding when you work to achieve them. Just as in making a refreshing cocktail... it starts with ice and goes up from there. Build a foundation and enjoy the outcome!

SIERRA
aka
SISI

Thank you to all the close friends and family in my life that have indulged this process and me by tasting the libations (not so forcefully), encouraging me and believing I could do this. Thank you to the wonderful man that is my husband... for ALL things. To my Mookie for passing along her passion and love of dogs and gift of creating recipes. To my dad for his taste buds. I am truly my parent's daughter.

To all the dogs in my life that fill and have filled me with so much happiness, love, purpose and... let's be honest... the need to create a cocktail from time to time! What a lucky girl I am!

Sara

CPSIA information can be obtained
at www.ICGtesting.com
Printed in the USA
LVHW082340220121
677171LV00005B/248

9 781735 172743